Everton

THE OFFICIAL EVERTON ANNUAL 2011

Written by Darren Griffiths & Adam Clark

Designed by Brian Thomson

A Grange Publication

© 2010. Published by Grange Communications Ltd., Edinburgh under licence from Everton Football Club.

Printed in the EU.

ISBN: 978-1-907104-63-3

£7.99

NIL SATIS NISI OPTIMUM

Everton

CONTENTS

DAVID MOYES

In February 2010 David Moyes was involved in his 600th match as a football manager and in March 2011, he will celebrate his 9th anniversary as Everton manager.

It was the spring of 2002 when the Glaswegian breezed into Goodison Park after being prised away from Preston North End and in typical fashion, Moyes wasted no time in stamping his mark on the club.

Within minutes of his first press conference he described Everton as being 'The People's Club' and then two days later he led the team for the first time and watched as they took the lead after 32 seconds against Fulham!

Since then, Moyes has made sure that Everton are no longer regarded merely as Premier League also-rans. The team has regularly finished in the top six, thus qualifying for Europe, and the League Cup semi-final as well as, of course, the FA Cup final have been reached.

On top of that, Moyes has won three Manager of the Year awards and seven Manager of the Month accolades - a figure bettered only by Sir Alex Ferguson and Arsene Wenger.

In short, he's done a great job since swapping Deepdale for Goodison but his philosophy has never changed; you only get out of it what you put into it.

There is no easy way to be successful – it's all about hard work.

Brilliant signings like Tim Cahill and Phil Jagielka don't just fall into his lap – the manager does extensive homework and refuses to leave any stone unturned in his bid to get the best players at the best prices for Everton Football Club.

"I said when I came into management that every player I sign, I want to see," he says.

"I'll watch videos but unless I've seen them live, I won't take them – and I haven't changed. It's what I do. I put my hours in and if that means taking a bit more time, I'm going to do it. If I miss a player because of that, so be it. There are times when I am abroad three times in a week and, by the end of those weeks, I can be on my knees physically. But when Everton make a signing I think we get scrutinised more because we don't have as much cash as some other clubs. Every penny I spend here becomes very precious."

In these days of knee–jerk reactions by chairmen and a real pressure to get results, not many managers will ever get to 600 games and for Moyes to do so at a comparatively young age is a wonderful achievement.

Typically though, he played it down!

"I am really fortunate that I had someone at Preston who gave me a chance to be a manager and had faith in me," he recalled. "Then Bill Kenwright had the faith in me to give me the job at Everton so I hope they would think their decisions have been the right ones – but for me every game still feels like the first one. I am still nervous, still keen to do well and I want a good Saturday night rather than a bad one!"

Thanks to David Moyes' efforts over the last eight–and–a–half years, Everton supporters have tended to be smiling rather than frowning on a Saturday night!

GOODISON MATCH DAY

Have you ever wondered what the build-up to a big game is like at Goodison Park? We take a behind-the-scenes look at the day Everton played Manchester United at Goodison Park last season and won 3-1!

One of the many programme sellers hoping to attract the attention of some of the early arrivals

→

The fans start to swarm around Goodison as the atmosphere builds up

↓

David Moyes happily signs an autograph in the stadium reception area before making his way through to the dressing room

→

Steven Pienaar poses for a photograph with a very happy Everton mascot

Landon Donovan listens to his favourite tunes on his ipod on his way into the dressing room

...before Alan Smith takes his position in the Goodison gantry, high above the Upper Bullens Stand.

The 'live' television commentators Alan Smith, Andy Gray and Rob Hawthorne share a joke in the tunnel whilst waiting for the teams to be announced...

Nearly time for kick–off!

The two captains prepare to give the referee their teamsheets. Haven't they met before?

The players go through their warm–up routine half an hour before the match starts

Anxious moments for David Moyes and Sir Alex Ferguson

Jack Rodwell celebrates his goal that seals a memorable victory for the Blues

Diniyar Bilyaletdinov tells the televison cameras what it was like to score a 25-yard screamer past Edwin van der Sar

Leon Osman happily accepts his Man of the Match award in the Sponsors' Lounge after the match

DINIYAR BILYALETDINOV

Diniyar Bilyaletdinov won the official Everton Goal of the Season award for 2009/10 for his stunning Goodison Park equaliser against Manchester United. The Russian midfielder smashed an unstoppable drive past a helpless Edwin van der Sar and it was the strike that won the fans vote as the best Everton goal of the campaign.

He duly received his award at the glittering ceremony in the Liverpool Cathedral and then a few days later he scored another fantastic goal that many felt was better than his United effort! Time was ebbing away against Portsmouth on the very last day of the season when Bilyaletdinov curled an absolutely superb shot into the top corner of the net from 25 yards.

Even the man himself rated it above the goal he won the award for!

"I think that goal was more beautiful than my goal against Manchester United," he said. "The guys have all told me it was amazing. The Manchester United goal was more important but the Portsmouth one was great because we wanted to win for the fans."

David Moyes was just as enthusiastic!

"I thought it was a stunning goal, an absolutely stunning goal," said the manager. "It was out of the blue, something out of nothing and it was just a top finish."

It was certainly a spectacular way to sign off his first season at Everton and the man who (thankfully!) is happy to be called 'Billy' hopes there's more to come.

"I want to score more goals for Everton and get more assists," he continued. "It is a very big part of my job and hopefully I can get more goals that are the same for the fans. I want to make them happy."

So what about the goal that won Bilyaletdinov the seasonal award?

The Toffees were trailing Manchester United at Goodison in February after Dimitar Berbatov had given the visitors a 15th– minute lead. But just three minutes later 'Billy' launched a Russian Rocket that flashed past the keeper and into the net.

Goodison was stunned, van der Sar was stunned, and so, to a certain extent, was the goalscorer!

"It was a surprise for me," he smiled. "I haven't scored a lot of great goals so it was a surprise. I just hope it's not my last against Manchester United."

Despite having to adapt to a whole new way of life after joining Everton from Lokomotiv Moscow, Bilyaletdinov enjoyed a very productive first season in English football, scoring seven goals.

THE RUSSIAN WITH THE ROCKET

David Moyes, who signed him for £10m, was very pleased with his goals return.

"He scored some really good goals last season but I'm not surprised because we'd watched him in Russia," said the boss. "He's a tremendous volleyer of the ball and we can see that in training; left foot or right foot he's got great technique. The goals he got last season were important for us and, I think, important for him as well to help him settle. "

Let's all keep our fingers crossed and hope there's more to come!!

PLAYER PROFILES

TIM HOWARD

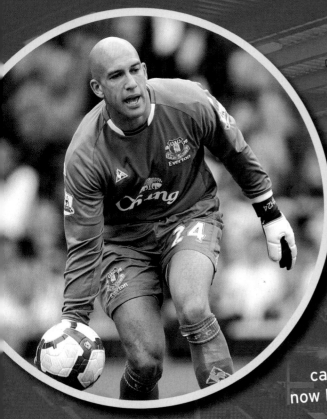

USA international Howard has been Everton's first-choice goalkeeper since moving to Goodison Park from Manchester United in the summer of 2006. Initially joining on loan, the deal was made permanent in February 2007 and the agile stopper has since gone on to make over 175 appearances for the Blues, breaking numerous Club records. Born in New Jersey, he began his career with his local side, MetroStars, now known as New York Red Bulls.

JAN MUCHA

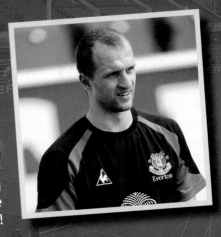

Mucha joined Everton from Legia Warsaw in July 2010. Brought in to battle with Tim Howard for a place in David Moyes' first team, the Blues actually sealed a deal to sign the Slovakian international in January but allowed him to stay with the Polish side until after the World Cup. Having won two Slovakian league titles with MSK Zilina and the Polish championship with Legia, Jan is now hoping to prove he has what it takes to make it in the Premier League!

IAIN TURNER

Highly-rated stopper Turner arrived at Everton from Scottish Third Division side Stirling Albion in January 2003 following a successful trial. A former Scotland Under-21 international, Iain has since had loan spells at six clubs, including Crystal Palace, Sheffield Wednesday and Nottingham Forest. He has made six first-team appearances for the Blues, the first as a late substitute in a 4-1 FA Cup fourth round defeat to Chelsea at Stamford Bridge in February 2006.

LEIGHTON BAINES

England international Baines joined Everton from Wigan Athletic just a few days before the start of the 2007/08 season. Having been on the Blues' books as a youngster, he returned to Goodison Park after a successful five-year spell with the Latics and this year surpassed 100 outings for the Club. Leighton made his Three Lions' debut in a 3–1 win over Egypt in March 2010 and was also named Everton's Players' Player of the Season for 2009/10!

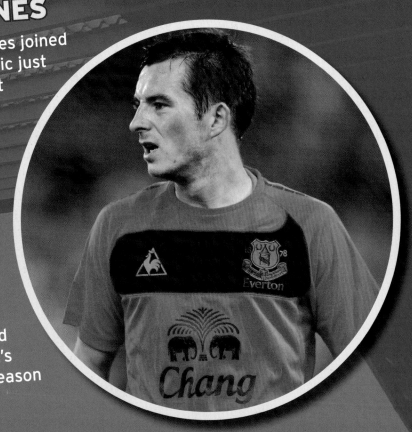

TONY HIBBERT

Renowned by many as the best tackler at the Club, Academy graduate Hibbert has forged an impressive career with Everton. Originally a midfield player, the Liverpool-born star is now a top quality right back who has racked up over 250 appearances for the Blues. In December 2009, Tony broke Everton's record for appearances in Europe, surpassing the 19 made by legendary duo Brian Labone and Colin Harvey.

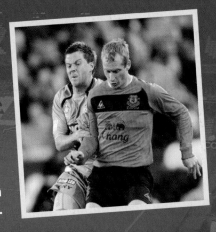

JOSEPH YOBO

Pacy centre back Yobo joined Everton, declining offers from Arsenal and Juventus, to become David Moyes' first signing in the summer of 2002. His switch to Merseyside followed spells in Belgium with Standard Liege, France with Marseille and Spain on loan at Tenerife. A Nigerian international with over 60 caps, Joe has played over 250 times in his eight-and-a-half years with the Toffees.

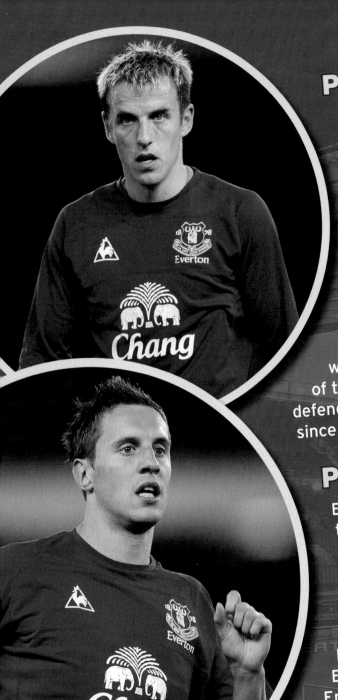

PHIL NEVILLE

England international Neville arrived at Goodison in August 2005 having won nearly every trophy possible during an 11-year spell with Manchester United. An England international with over 50 caps, Phil collected six Premier League titles, three FA Cups and a Champions League during his time at Old Trafford! A committed, hard-working and inspirational member of the squad, the midfielder (or defender!) has been Everton's captain since January 2007.

PHIL JAGIELKA

Everton's Player of the Season for the 2008/09 campaign, Jagielka has been at Everton since joining from relegated Sheffield United in the summer of 2007. A versatile player who can operate in central defence, at full back and in midfield, he is another who spent time on Everton's books as a teenager. An England international who made his debut against Trinidad and Tobago in June 2008, 'Jags' missed nearly seven months of the 2009/10 campaign due to a cruciate knee ligament problem.

JOHN HEITINGA

Dutch international Heitinga was a transfer deadline day signing last year when he arrived from Atletico Madrid for an initial fee of £6million. A player capable of performing either in midfield or defence, the no-nonsense operator brought a wealth of experience with him, having played for Ajax and Spanish giants Atletico Madrid. A successful first season in England followed his debut at Fulham in September 2009 and he went on to star for Holland last summer as the Dutch went all the way to the World Cup final.

SYLVAIN DISTIN

Calm and collected Frenchman Distin joined Everton from Portsmouth for an undisclosed fee in August 2009 and was a virtual ever-present during the 2009/10 campaign. Released by PSG as a teenager, he was later re-signed by the Ligue 1 giants after helping Gueugnon to a French League Cup triumph in 2000. He moved to England to join Newcastle on loan in 2001, later spending five years at Manchester City before moving to Fratton Park in 2007. Sylvain played 38 times for Everton during his first season at Goodison Park, getting himself on the scoresheet on two occasions!

SEAMUS COLEMAN

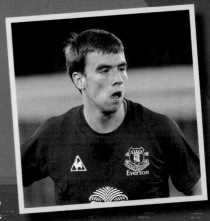

A Republic of Ireland Under-21 international, the Donegal-born full back signed for Everton at the end of the January transfer window in 2009, having attracted reported interest from Celtic, Birmingham City and Ipswich Town. A regular for the reserves during his first season at the Club, Seamus overcame a serious foot infection last summer to make his first-team debut against Benfica in October 2009. He then went on loan to Blackpool and helped the Seasiders reach the Premier League via the Championship play-off final at Wembley!

SHANE DUFFY

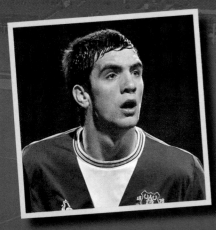

Everton signed Duffy as a highly-regarded 16-year-old from Northern Irish outfit Foyle Harps and the 6ft 4ins centre back has since become a regular feature in David Moyes' matchday squad. A former Northern Ireland Under-21 international, he changed his allegiance to the Republic of Ireland in February 2010 and was selected in a senior training squad in May. Sadly, Shane suffered a serious injury while away with his nation but it is hoped he will bounce back just as strong as before!

SHKODRAN MUSTAFI

Centre back Mustafi moved to Everton in the summer of 2009, joining from Hamburg. A player of Albanian descent, the German youth international worked mainly with the reserves during the 2009/10 campaign but made a handful of appearances on the first-team substitutes' bench and emerged for a short debut in a Europa League game against FC BATE Borisov!

PLAYING AGAINST THE BLUES

They may be regulars in Blue at Goodison Park – but that hasn't always been the case! Here's some of our current squad in action AGAINST Everton earlier in their careers...

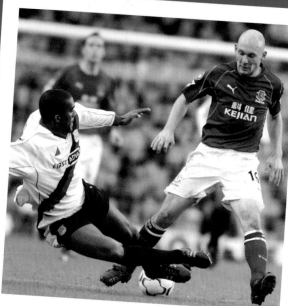

Sylvain Distin, then with Manchester City, puts a strong challenge in on Thomas Gravesen at Goodison

Yakubu challenging for the ball with Mikel Arteta when our striker played for Middlesbrough

Tim Howard shakes hands with Phil Neville at the end of an Everton v Manchester United match

Mikel Arteta in battle again –
this time with Sheffield United's
Phil Jagielka

Leighton Baines chases
Andy Johnson during his
Wigan Athletic days

Louis Saha brings the ball away from
Leon Osman at Old Trafford during
his spell at Manchester United

Phil Neville is in
the red of Manchester
United as he shields
the ball from
Tomasz Radzinski

19

JUNIOR QUIZ

SEE HOW MUCH YOU KNOW ABOUT YOUR FAVOURITE TEAM

Write your answers down on a piece of blank paper and see how many you get correct. Then challenge your Evertonian pals to see if they can do better!

1. Other than Celtic, name one of the Scottish League teams that David Moyes played for.

2. Against which team did Everton win a League Cup tie last season by 4-0?

3. Leighton Baines scored two penalties for Everton last season. Apart from the fact that they were both at the Park End, what else did they have in common?

4. From which French side did Everton sign Joseph Yobo?

5. What has Mikel Arteta got in common with Everton legend Andy Gray, current goalkeeping coach Chris Woods and former England hero Paul Gascoigne?

6. Against which two Premier League teams did Jermaine Beckford score cup goals during the 2009/10 season?

7. Which European city did Everton visit twice last season in the Europa League?

8. Against which two teams did Landon Donovan score last season?

9. Tim Howard is an honorary member of which world-famous sports team?

10. Which of the following teams has Steve Round NOT coached: Newcastle United, Leeds United, England or Middlesbrough?

11. One to think about - who was the last Everton player to score a European goal for the club?

12. True or false. Everton's final goal of last season was a stunning strike by Diniyar Bilyaletdinov that flew past Portsmouth's David James at the Gwladys Street end.

13. Since leaving Everton, who has had spells at Preston North End and Sheffield Wednesday?

14. Who was the last goalkeeper to concede a goal against Everton at Wembley?

15. Here's a tricky one to end with! Only four ex-Everton first-team players took part in the 2010 World Cup. Can you name them?

JACK RODWELL
Midfielder

evertonfc.com

YOU WILL HAVE ALREADY VISITED EVERTONFC.COM, THE CLUB'S OFFICIAL WEBSITE, FOR YOUR DAILY FIX OF NEWS, TO FIND OUT MORE ABOUT OUR LATEST SIGNINGS OR TO READ WHAT MANAGER DAVID MOYES AND HIS PLAYERS HAD TO SAY ABOUT OUR MOST RECENT VICTORY.

BUT HERE'S THE LOWDOWN ON SOME OF THE SECTIONS OF EVERTONFC.COM YOU MIGHT NOT HAVE FOUND YET...

KIDS ZONE

This is where there's plenty of Everton fun to be had! Put your knowledge of the Blues to the test with our Everton Quiz, brush up on your stats and facts with Did You Know or try to beat your record in our addictive virtual card game, Everton Snaps!

Visit **evertonfc.com/kidszone**

FAN MAP

This is our virtual world map which allows you to let every other Evertonian on the planet know exactly where you're supporting us from, whether it be from New York, Netherton, Melbourne or by the Mersey!

Visit **evertonfc.com/fanmap**

HISTORY TIMELINE

We've let you in on some of the greatest characters and stories from Everton's illustrious history in this year's annual but if you want to get one up on your Evertonian mates then why not check out our History Timeline to find out a little bit more? From our humble beginnings as St Domingo to our most recent achievements under David Moyes, this tool plots our history step-by-step in pictures and words!

Visit **evertonfc.com/historytimeline**

WALLPAPERS AND SCREENSAVERS

Why not show your true colours to all your friends and family by grabbing one of our wallpapers or screensavers? Featuring every member of Everton's current first-team squad, as well as some of the most iconic images of the Club's illustrious past, these free downloads are sure to make your laptop or computer the envy of Evertonians everywhere!

Visit **evertonfc.com/screensavers** and **evertonfc.com/wallpapers**

PODCASTS

Did Santa bring you a new iPod or iPhone this Christmas? Well, why not download the Official evertonfc.com Podcast? Our weekly shows let you in on all the secrets of Finch Farm, bringing you the latest news, plus exclusive interviews and features with your favourite Everton stars. With new podcasts uploaded every week, it's another great way to keep in touch with all the goings at your Club! And if you don't have a new gadget to listen on, don't panic!! You can listen to each and every podcast we produce online!

Visit **evertonfc.com/podcasts**

SEE THE STARS ON everton tv

DO **you know all the places evertonTV have been lucky enough to visit in the last year or so? It's some list!**

We followed David Moyes and his men across the length and breadth of the continent during last season's Europa League campaign, taking us to countries including Belarus, Greece and Portugal.

While there, we followed all the travelling Toffees to the major sights, filmed training and brought you exclusive pre and post-match interviews with the players and their manager.

We were also invited to travel to San Sebastian in northern Spain to spend the day with Mikel Arteta as he recovered from a knee injury. We went on a tour of the midfielder's home town, took in the pitches he played on as a boy and visited Anoeta, the stadium belonging to one of his former clubs, Real Sociedad.

Our cameras were also allowed to follow the Spaniard to see all the hard work and effort that goes into recovering from such a serious injury.

evertonTV also joined Steven Pienaar on a private jet to Zurich, the largest city in Switzerland and the home of FIFA. As the star player of 2010 World Cup hosts South Africa, our man was there to make the draw for the qualification play-offs and we were with him every step of the way, bringing you a detailed account of a whirlwind day which saw Steven and our cameramen back in Liverpool in time for tea!

These are all great examples of the kind of coverage Blues fans can only get by subscribing to evertonTV.

With exclusive interviews, fantastic features, news on the Reserves and Ladies, behind-the-scenes footage, plus extended highlights of every first-team game, evertonTV really is a must-have for supporters everywhere.

Throughout the season there will even be opportunities to become a star of evertonTV yourself so look out for those!

Keep up-to-date with all the goings-on both at Goodison Park and the Club's Finch Farm training ground and check out evertonTV today.

To find out how to subscribe visit evertonfc.com/evertonTV.

EVERTON
AT THE WORLD CUP

Where were you this summer? Glued to the television, no doubt!

And who can blame you? All the very best players from around the globe were on display as Africa played host to the game's greatest tournament, the World Cup, for the very first time.

Everton had no less than seven stars out there, representing six different nations - including the hosts and the runners-up!

JOHN HEITINGA: HOLLAND

What a World Cup it was for Johnny Heitinga! The defender played every game as the Netherlands went all the way to the final! Japan, Denmark and Cameroon were all easily brushed aside in Group E, Jan Mucha's Slovakia were beaten in the last 16 and they even slayed giants Brazil! The 3-2 win over Uruguay in the semis was another highlight and, though Spain eventually took the trophy, it was an unforgettable tournament for Johnny and his Oranje pals!

STEVEN PIENAAR: SOUTH AFRICA

This was always going to be a big competition for Steven Pienaar being the star player of the host nation. A 1-1 draw in the tournament opener gave Bafana Bafana hope of escaping a tough Group A but a 3-0 loss to Uruguay left them with too big a mountain to climb. The tournament did end on a high note though - they defeated the mighty France 2-1 to knock them out too! And another thing - their supporters were brilliant! Who will ever forget the colour in the stands and the noise of the vuvuzelas!?!

TIM HOWARD: USA

Thanks to their spirited never-say-die attitude, the USA attracted some of the craziest crowds and – for the summer at least – had everyone in the States buzzing about 'soccer'! After England's Rob Green gifted them a point in their opening game, the Americans came from two goals down to draw with Slovakia before a late Landon Donovan goal defeated Algeria and saw the States top Group C. Sadly for Tim and his team-mates their run ended with a 2–1 loss to Ghana in the last 16 – though they were arguably the better team that night!

TIM CAHILL: AUSTRALIA

Mr Dependable for club and country, Everton's Aussie bounced back from a controversial sending off in Australia's first Group D clash against Germany to head home the opening goal in the Socceroos' 2–1 win over fancied Serbia. The madly-celebrated win wasn't enough to book a place in the latter stages though and Cahill and co headed home early. Despite that, our man was the star of the show in the two games he played - and is was fantastic to see him on the scoresheet too!

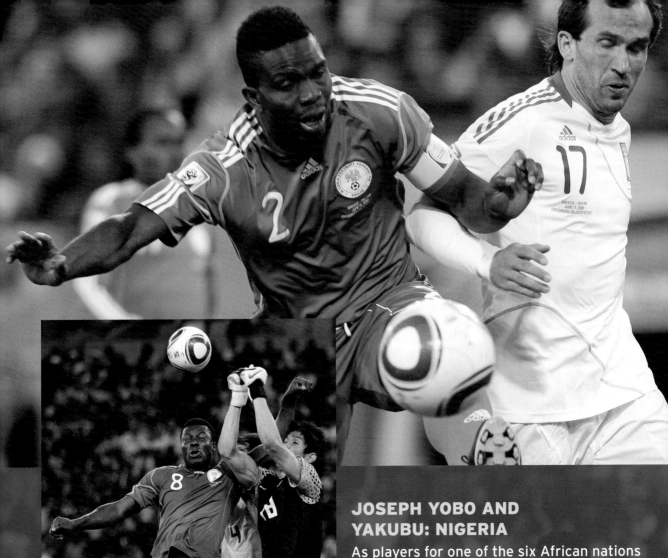

JOSEPH YOBO AND YAKUBU: NIGERIA

As players for one of the six African nations involved in the tournament is was always going to be a memorable summer for Yakubu and Joseph Yobo. Sadly, an impressive display against Lionel Messi and his Argentine team-mates couldn't prevent Nigeria starting out with a 1–0 defeat, and a second loss against Greece meant they had it all to do in their final game against South Korea. Trailing 2–1 with just 21 minutes to go, Yak gave them hope from the penalty spot but the Super Eagles just couldn't find the winner they needed to soar into the next round!

JAN MUCHA: SLOVAKIA

All Evertonian eyes were on Jan Mucha at the World Cup as everyone knew the giant stopper was heading to Goodison Park as soon as the competition finished. And he didn't disappoint! In fact, the Slovakians were among the tournament's overachievers, finishing ahead of New Zealand and the then reigning champions Italy to set up a last 16 clash with Holland. The eventual finalists proved a little too much for the European minnows though and - despite some heroics from our man Jan - a 2–1 defeat brought an end to their World Cup dream.

WORDSEARCH

IT'S TRAINING DAY AT FINCH FARM. CAN YOU FIND THESE 12 TRAINING-RELATED WORDS IN THE GRID BELOW:

A	I	V	P	P	X	Q	R	E	N	K	X	S	F	Z	Z
C	V	N	W	Y	Z	S	Z	L	F	T	M	B	W	B	S
A	X	F	U	S	G	G	U	G	D	O	Y	F	T	A	W
D	O	V	B	D	Z	Y	T	S	O	N	V	R	X	L	I
E	Q	Q	C	N	P	I	M	R	I	O	S	G	B	L	M
M	B	W	T	S	M	H	G	N	N	L	L	O	V	W	M
Y	L	R	B	O	M	N	Y	I	A	T	L	A	W	O	I
Z	Z	I	O	H	I	A	X	S	V	S	O	L	F	R	N
D	B	J	K	G	P	P	G	G	I	L	I	S	T	K	G
P	I	I	N	Y	D	N	C	I	Y	O	D	U	A	C	P
F	R	A	Z	U	I	U	O	I	F	Y	R	L	M	P	O
M	H	I	K	N	Z	R	N	A	B	O	Q	O	D	V	O
C	N	G	N	O	C	Z	E	Y	E	L	K	K	O	R	L
G	B	U	W	F	F	F	S	E	L	I	Q	W	Z	M	D
H	R	F	I	N	C	H	F	A	R	M	V	P	L	Y	J
F	R	A	S	T	R	O	T	U	R	F	J	D	A	A	D

FINCH FARM

SWIMMING POOL

CONES

GOALS

ACADEMY

RUNNING

BALL WORK

GYMNASIUM

PHYSIO ROOM

BIBS

CHANGING ROOMS

ASTROTURF

Answers on Page 61

27

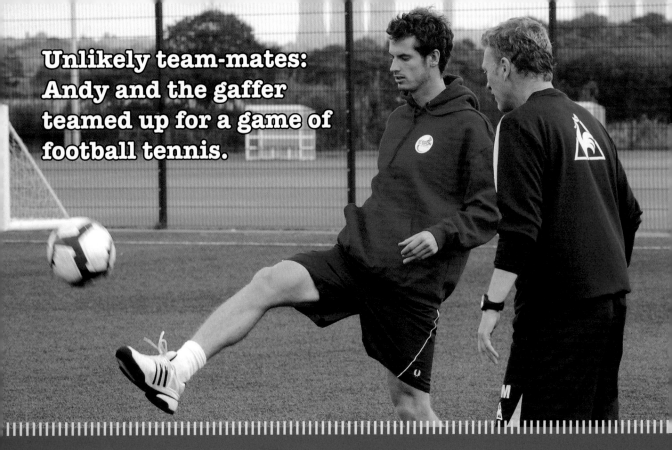

Unlikely team-mates: Andy and the gaffer teamed up for a game of football tennis.

MURRAY SWINGS BY

David Moyes gives his fellow Scotsman the Finch Farm tour!

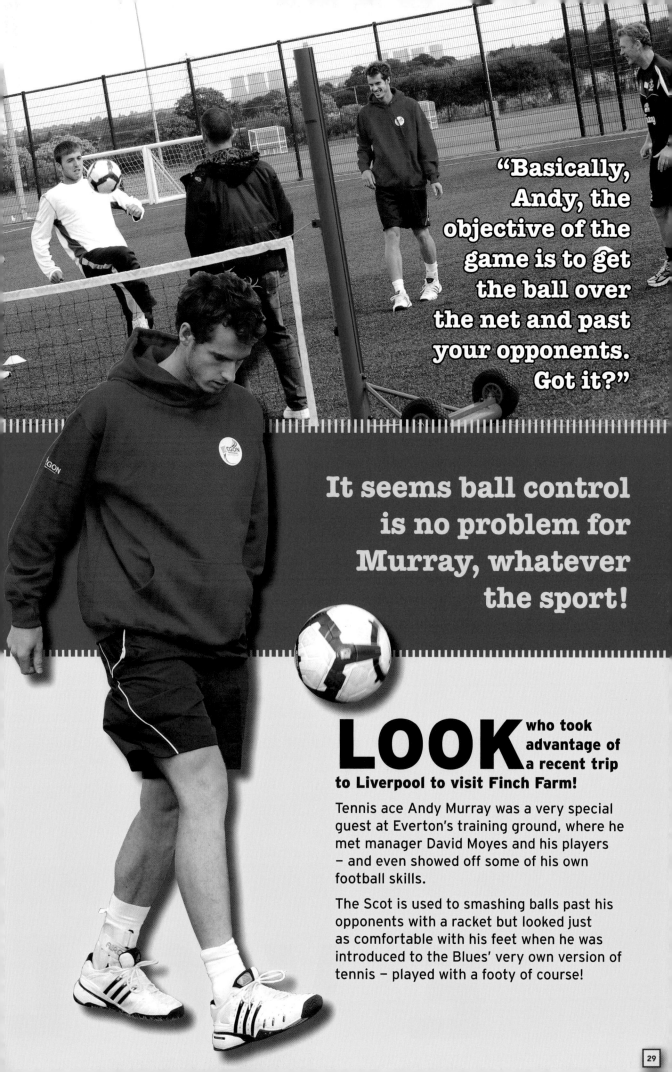

"Basically, Andy, the objective of the game is to get the ball over the net and past your opponents. Got it?"

It seems ball control is no problem for Murray, whatever the sport!

LOOK who took advantage of a recent trip to Liverpool to visit Finch Farm!

Tennis ace Andy Murray was a very special guest at Everton's training ground, where he met manager David Moyes and his players – and even showed off some of his own football skills.

The Scot is used to smashing balls past his opponents with a racket but looked just as comfortable with his feet when he was introduced to the Blues' very own version of tennis – played with a footy of course!

REVOL

U T I O N

The Blues take a stroll past the famous Sydney Opera House

BLUES DOWN UNDER

The team arrive in Sydney

ONE of the most important parts of any season is the preparation – meaning David Moyes always thinks long and hard about where he wants to take his players on tour.

After a succession of trips to America, the Blues boss decided Australia would be the destination for this summer's getaway and, as our snaps show, the players did everything they could to make the most of their time Down Under!

Moyes' men took on A-League sides Sydney FC, Melbourne Heart and Brisbane Roar and beat them all to return home with a 100 per cent record!

But, having travelled thousands of miles to be there, the jet-setting Blues also took the chance to take in all the sights and sounds of the three cities they were lucky enough to visit. What's more, they invited our cameras along for the ride...

Phil Neville and Leon Osman lift the Roars Against Racism Trophy after beating Brisbane 2–1

ROARS AGAINST RACISM CUP

Changy enjoyed his holidays!

evertonTV interview Aussie cricket legend Brett Lee

A CAREER IN PICTURES...
MAROUANE FELLAINI

He may still be a young man but Marouane Fellaini has already packed a lot of football into his career so far.

Born in Belgium, Fellaini spent a few years at the Academy of Anderlecht but his first professional club was Standard Liege. He made a quick impression and it wasn't long before he was picked to play international football for Belgium.

In the summer of 2008 he joined Everton for a club record fee of £15m...

Fellaini in action against Brazil during the 2008 Olympic Games

Chasing the ball with Fernando Torres during a Champions League match for Standard Liege against Liverpool

Battling for the ball with Portugal's Tiago during a 2007 international match

Fighting for possession on his Everton debut away at Stoke City

Lashing home another goal for the Blues! This time against Sunderland in the Premier League

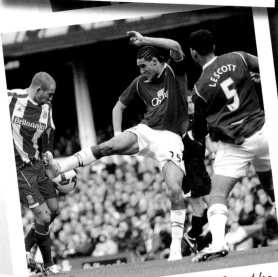

A change of hairstyle for the visit of Stoke City in 2009...but the braids didn't last long!

A young Fellaini poses for a picture at Standard Liege

An injury against Liverpool brings an end to his 2009/10 season

IF YOU KNOW YOUR HISTORY...

William Ralph 'Dixie' Dean takes to the field for Everton

EVERTON'S

history began in 1878 when we played our first match in the south-east corner of Liverpool's Stanley Park. Back then we weren't known as Everton but St Domingo, so named after the church which provided the players for the side.

Our first game as Everton Football Club took place just over a year later, on 20 December 1879, at Stanley Park. We played a team called St Peter's and ran out 6–0 winners!

Soon after we moved to a new ground on Priory Road and later another one on Anfield Road. And you know who that patch of land belongs to now!

It does mean, though, that, on 8 September 1888, our first ever League match was played at Anfield. It proved lucky for us that day as we defeated Accrington 2–1 to kick off the first ever Football League campaign with a victory!

Three years later, we won our first League title, becoming only the second club to win the championship (Preston North End won the first two!) but the owner of the Anfield site doubled the rent on his land and the Everton committee decided to move again.

Within a few months the Club were installed at Goodison Park - England's first purpose–built football stadium. It was first used on 24 August 1892, with 12,000 spectators turning up for the grand opening.

During the 1890s, Everton lost two FA Cup finals and it wasn't until 1906 that the famous trophy finally ended up in our hands thanks to a 1–0 win over Newcastle United.

In 1914/15, we clinched the Football League title again and the outbreak of World War I left the side as champions for four years!

The next historical chapter for the Club began in 1924/25 with the signing of a Tranmere Rovers youngster called William Ralph 'Dixie' Dean.

In Dean's first full season – 1925/26 – he scored 32 league goals in 38 games. In his next he netted 21 in 27 and then, in 1927/28, he created history. SIXTY league goals in 39 matches is a record that will surely stand for eternity - though it required a last day hat–trick against Arsenal at Goodison to ensure the mark was reached. It was also enough to see Everton end the season as champions once again!

Astonishingly, we suffered relegation before more top honours were added to our trophy cabinet as, two seasons later, we finished bottom of the table and were condemned to the second tier of English football for the first time.

Predictably, Dean was unstoppable in Division Two and he smashed 39 league goals in just 37 appearances as Everton stormed back to the top flight at the first time of asking. The very next season – 1931/32 – the Blues regained the First Division title, with Dean adding another 45 league goals to his tally!

The title was followed with a memorable FA Cup triumph in 1933 – the Club's first at Wembley - thanks to a 3–0 thumping of Manchester City. Dean became Everton's first ever No 9 that afternoon as shirt numbers were introduced to the English game.

The great Dean had departed by the time the league title was regained in 1938/39 but - and not for the first time – the outbreak of war halted Everton's progress.

League football resumed in 1946 but, four years later, the Blues were relegated once more and endured three long seasons outside the top flight.

Three years later, with that man Catterick still at the helm, we were part of one of the FA Cup's most dramatic ever finals. Two-nil down to Sheffield Wednesday with just over 30 minutes to go, a young Cornishman called Mike Trebilcock scored twice in quick succession to level before the legendary Derek Temple fired an Everton winner to bring the Cup back to Goodison!

Manager Harry Catterick in 1961

It wasn't until we appointed former player Harry Catterick as manager in April 1961 that our fortunes really turned around again. At the end of his first full season in charge the Club finished fourth and boasted the First Division's best defensive record. The next year we lost just six of our 42 matches and won the title six points clear of our nearest rivals, Tottenham Hotspur!

Captain Brian Labone poses with the FA Cup in 1966

The Blues celebrate the 1966 FA Cup triumph at Wembley

Howard Kendall returned to the Club in 1981, this time as a manager, and after a slow start, the team rallied and, from the depths of despair, rose to heights they had never dared dream about.

Graeme Sharp scores in the 1984 FA Cup final

The great Alan Ball made 251 appearances for The Toffees

By now Catterick had some of the best players of the generation at his disposal and, sure enough, in 1969/70 it all came together in one glorious Championship campaign; a team inspired by Howard Kendall, Alan Ball and Colin Harvey – a trio of midfielders known as 'The Holy Trinity' – ending the campaign nine points clear at the top of the table!

Following that triumph, all Evertonians prepared themselves for a decade of glory, but it never materialised. The only real highlight of the 1970s was the emergence of Bob Latchford, a centre forward who scored 30 league goals during the 1977/78 season, scooping a £10,000 prize from a national newspaper in the process. And Bob will tell you, that was an incredible amount of money in those days!

In 1984, we secured our first piece of silverware in over a decade with a 2–0 victory over Watford in the FA Cup final and the next campaign –1984/85 – was a season like none before, and none since. Kendall's men stormed to the title with a record 90-point haul – 13 clear of second-placed Liverpool. On top of that, we tasted success in Europe for the first time, defeating Austria's Rapid Vienna 3–1 in Rotterdam to lift the European Cup Winners' Cup.

Howard Kendall returned as manager in 1981

Kevin Sheedy shows off the 1985 League Championship trophy

The golden era continued as the Blues took the league title again in 1986/87 but Kendall's successor – his one-time team-mate, Colin Harvey – could not find the formula to continue our success into the 1990s.

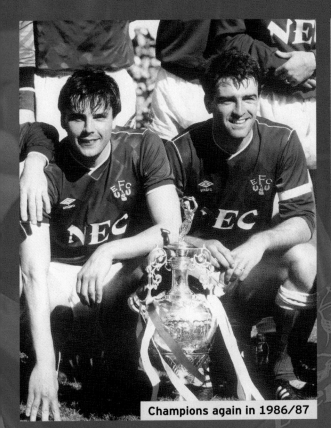

Champions again in 1986/87

SO, DO YOU DO KNOW YOUR HISTORY... ?

Were you paying attention to all that? Let's see if you can answer all these questions about our great football club without reading back...

1. When did Everton's history begin?

2. In which season did we win our first League title?

3. How was William Ralph Dean better known?

4. Who was the manager who led Everton to an FA Cup win in 1966? And by what scoreline did we beat Sheffield Wednesday at Wembley?

5. By what name were the trio of Howard Kendall, Alan Ball and Colin Harvey known?

6. Who won £10,000 for scoring 30 league goals in the 1977/78 season?

7. Which trophy did we win by beating Rapid Vienna 3–1 in 1985?

8. Name the player who scored our FA Cup winning goal against Manchester United in 1995?

9. Who did David Moyes replace as Everton manager?

10. Who did we play in the 2009 FA Cup final?

A second stint in charge for Kendall and an ill-fated spell for Mike Walker followed, before Joe Royle, another man who had starred for Everton in his playing days, finally earned us another trophy with a 1–0 win over Manchester United in the 1995 FA Cup final. As we had only narrowly escaped relegation from what was by now the Premier League, Alex Ferguson's side were massive favourites that day but Paul Rideout headed the only goal to spark wild celebrations at the Blue end of Wembley!

The following campaign did not quite go to plan for our FA Cup winners though, and by the end of the 1996/97 season, Royle had gone. Kendall returned again but his third spell at the helm almost ended in disaster – we only avoided relegation on the very last day of the season!

Kendall was replaced by Glasgow Rangers boss Walter Smith and, while stability returned, the Scotsman's reign came to an end when relegation again loomed in the spring of 2002.

That paved the way for David Moyes to step in. In his first top-flight role, the former Preston boss guided Everton away from the drop zone and in eight full seasons since, he has led us to European qualification on four occasions, famously securing a top-four finish in 2005.

The 2007/08 campaign saw our most successful European excursion for 23 years, as we reached the last 16 of the UEFA Cup (now the Europa League) and, in 2009, we returned to Wembley for the first time in 14 years, narrowly losing out to Chelsea in a closely-fought FA Cup final.

Injuries looked to have put paid to Moyes' quest to again secure European football last term but the Blues bounced back brilliantly in the second half of the campaign, narrowly missing out on a Europa League spot in the final weeks of the season.

David Moyes greets Everton fans for the first time in 2002

EVERTON'S 2009/10 PLAYERS' PLAYER OF THE YEAR WAS...
LEIGHTON BAINES

The popular defender had a terrific season and was rewarded at the magnificent Liverpool Anglican Cathedral with the biggest compliment a player can get - being voted the campaign's best player by all his team-mates.

"That was without doubt the biggest individual award I have won in my whole time as a footballer," said Baines.

"To be acknowledged by your colleagues, the players you work and train with every day, is as good as it gets. I'm just proud to play for Everton and to play alongside world-class players week-in and week-out and for them to vote for me was unbelievable. I actually voted for Steve Pienaar because I thought he had an exceptional season."

The sheer quality and consistency that Baines showed throughout a season that began badly for the team but finished very strongly just made Fabio Capello's decision not to take him to the World Cup all the more baffling.

After forcing his way into the reckoning, Baines was then surprisingly left out of the final squad for South Africa and it was a decision that really disappointed him.

"Of course it did," he said. "Everyone wants to play for their country in a World Cup and for me to get so close was very disappointing. I actually thought I'd done enough and I felt confident that I wouldn't let anyone down but the manager had a difficult decision to make and at least he was honest with all the lads he didn't pick. He knew we were gutted about it but he approached us in a very professional and courteous manner and that's all you can ask for. Football will always bring its ups and downs and it's just about how you cope with them."

At least Baines had the consolation of knowing that he would be fully rested ahead of what could yet be an exciting season for Everton. Only two defeats from December 2009 until the end of the last campaign gave the supporters plenty of optimism ahead of the new season. It's a feeling of expectation that the players shared.

"We knew that if we'd had a full squad of players from the start of last season then we would certainly have qualified for the Europa League or maybe even the Champions League," he reckoned. "You could see when Mikel and Jags came back into the team that we instantly looked stronger and don't forget that we lost Steven Pienaar, Phil Neville and Leon Osman for large parts of the season and any team would miss players of their

quality. But with everyone fit and available we looked instantly stronger and I think this is definitely the strongest we've been since I joined the club."

Away from the pitch, Baines was Everton Football Club's Premier League Reading Star for the 2009/10 season. It's a role he thoroughly enjoyed.

"I think it's a great scheme," he said. "Basically, every team selects a Reading Star who picks his favourite book and encourages children to use their local library and get more out of reading. I picked a book by John Grisham, called an Innocent Man."

2010 AWARDS

Everton's 5th Annual End of Season Awards evening took place in May 2010 in the magnificent setting of the Liverpool Anglican Cathedral.

The event was presented by one of television's most recognizable sports faces, Steve Rider, and was attended by David Moyes, his staff and the entire first–team squad.

As usual, there was a plethora of awards to get through on the night and many people associated with Everton Football Club were honoured for their contributions.

A host of ex–Everton stars, including Ian Snodin, Ronny Goodlass, Derek Temple and Duncan McKenzie were also in attendance and it was another memorable night.

Bill Kenwright made a passionate speech about the club and introduced his own special 'Chairman's Blueblood Award' which went jointly to the two Tims - Cahill and Howard!

The Life Vice President of the Club, Mr Keith Tamlin, was recognised for his loyalty with a special 'Contribution Award' and there were personal honours for players from the Reserve, Academy, Disabled and Ladies teams.

Jack Rodwell receives his Young Player of the Season award from the presenter, Steve Rider

Steven Pienaar poses for photographs after receiving the Player of the Season award

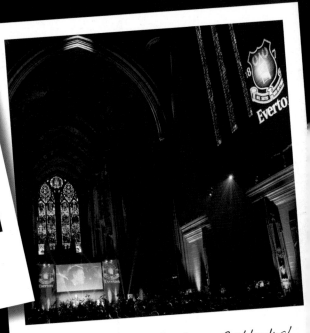

The Liverpool Anglican Cathedral is 'blue' for the night!

Tim Cahill and Tim Howard celebrate their Chairman's Blueblood Award with Bill Kenwright

Maroune Fellaini arrives at the ceremony

The manager is all smiles as he makes his way into the cathedral

David Moyes tells Steve Rider all about the excellent finish to the season

PLAYER PROFILES

MIKEL ARTETA

Skilful and versatile Spaniard Arteta has become a firm fans' favourite since joining Everton, initially on loan, from Real Socieded in January 2005. 'Mikky' began his career with Barcelona and has also had spells at PSG and Glasgow Rangers, where he won the Scottish title. A serious knee problem sustained in February 2009 led to an 11-month injury lay-off for the midfielder but he wasted little time in reminding Evertonians what they'd been missing with some dazzling displays in 2010! He then put smiles on everyone's faces by agreeing a new five-year contact in the summer!

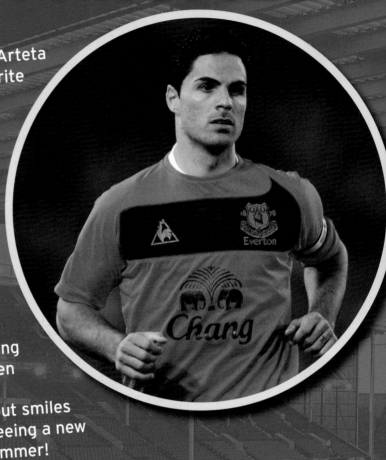

JAKE BIDWELL

Left back Bidwell has been at Everton since the age of 11. He signed scholarship forms in the summer of 2009 and was handed a first-team debut in the Europa League dead rubber against FC BATE Borisov in December 2009. Aged just 16 years and 271 days, he became the youngest person to ever represent the Club in Europe!

DINIYAR BILYALETDINOV

Russian international Bilyaletdinov joined Everton from Lokomotiv Moscow for an undisclosed fee in August 2009. The winger, who arrived aged 24, broke into Lokomotiv's first team in 2004, quickly forging a reputation for his direct running style and the leadership skills which would later be rewarded with the captain's armband. A regular for his international side, he settled quickly into life on Merseyside, scoring seven goals in 33 games during a successful first season in England.

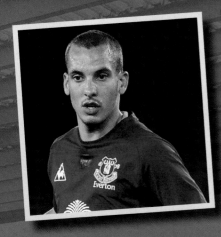

LEON OSMAN

Another player to have risen through the Academy ranks, Osman was part of the Everton team which won the FA Youth Cup in 1998. His dreams of becoming a professional footballer were almost shattered in 2001 when he suffered a serious knee injury but successful loan spells at Carlisle United and Derby County saw him eventually force his way into David Moyes' first-team plans. Unquestionably Everton's prankster, 'Ossie' enjoyed arguably his best ever season in 2009/10.

JAMES WALLACE

Liverpool-born Wallace joined Everton's Academy aged 13. A goalscoring midfielder, he is comfortable in possession and impressed enough in his outings for the Under-18s and reserves to be handed a first-team debut against Czech outfit Sigma Olomouc in August 2009. A regular presence on David Moyes' bench in the past two seasons, much is hoped of our England youth international.

MAROUANE FELLAINI

Belgian international Fellaini became Everton's record signing on transfer deadline day in September 2008 when he joined the Club in a £15million move from homeland side Standard Liege. Quickly drawing attention due to his height and 'afro' hairstyle, 'Felli' became an instant cult hero and scooped the Club's Young Player of the Year award in his first season. Unfortunately, an even brighter 2009/10 campaign was cut short by an ankle injury sustained in February but no Evertonian is ever likely to forget the turn which bamboozled Manchester City's Craig Bellamy!

TIM CAHILL

Sydney-born Cahill joined Everton from Millwall in the summer of 2005 in a move he described as 'a dream come true'. A forceful, strong-running midfielder, he is remarkably talented in the air and this year surpassed the 50-goal mark for the Club. The first Australian to score in a World Cup finals, Tim has been a virtual ever-present since making the switch to Goodison Park and is another firm fans' favourite. And he signed a new four-year contract in May!

JACK RODWELL

Starlet Rodwell made his full Everton debut as a substitute against AZ Alkmaar at the age of just 16 years and 284 days to become the youngest ever person to play for the Blues in Europe! Though that record has since been taken by Jake Bidwell, England Under-21 international Jack has become a first-team regular at Goodison and has already made well over 50 senior appearances. And expect many more - our bright young talent put pen to paper on a new long-term contract in May!

HOPE AKPAN

Liverpool-born Akpan has been a regular for Everton's Academy side since first appearing against Liverpool at the age of 15. A tough-tackling central midfielder, he became a reserve-team regular during the 2008/09 campaign and was handed a first-team debut from the bench in a Europa League clash with FC BATE Borisov in December 2009!

JOSE BAXTER

Striker Baxter has been at Everton since he was just six-years-old! A player of immense natural talent he can also perform in midfield and has regularly represented England at youth level. And did you know, his late substitute appearance against Blackburn Rovers in August 2008 saw him become the Club's youngest first-team player at just 16 years and 191 days old?

JERMAINE BECKFORD

When Beckford's contract at Leeds United came to an end in May 2010, Everton beat a host of other clubs to secure his signature. The striker was a key figure in the Elland Road side's promotion to the Championship last term, impressing David Moyes with his 31 goals in all competitions – including the one which knocked Manchester United out of the FA Cup! And did you know, Jermaine was playing non-league football for Wealdstone until Leeds spotted him in 2006?

KIERAN AGARD

Jet-heeled striker Agard joined Everton's Academy from Arsenal midway through the 2005/06 season. He has since progressed through the ranks to the fringes of the first-team and was rewarded with a senior bow as a substitute at Hull City in September 2009. Further late run-outs followed but the youngster's 2009/10 campaign was cruelly ended when a knee problem left him needing surgery. Look out for him again in 2011!

STEVEN PIENAAR

Crafty playmaker Pienaar joined Everton, initially on loan, from German outfit Borussia Dortmund in the summer of 2007. Having emerged as one of the hottest talents at Ajax's feeder club, Ajax Cape Town, the attack-minded midfielder was signed by the Dutch giants in 2001 and played in a side which also included Zlatan Ibrahimovic and John Heitinga before moving to Dortmund in 2006. In 2010, Steven made his 100th appearance for the Blues and starred for hosts South Africa at the World Cup!

OSSIE'S SIX OF THE BEST!

Leon Osman has played more than 200 games for Everton since making his debut against Tottenham Hotspur in 2002. He's played in many big matches in League, Cup and Europe and scored some memorable goals along the way.

A product of the Everton Youth Academy and a Goodison Park favourite, 'Ossie' takes a look back now at the Top Six most memorable games of his career so far...

TOTTENHAM HOTSPUR v EVERTON 2003

This was my Everton debut - although I didn't even know I was in the squad until just before the kick-off! Richard Wright injured himself during the warm-up so our on-loan keeper, Espen Baardsen had to take over, which meant we were one short on the bench so the manager told me I'd be one of the substitutes! I came on for the last few minutes as a replacement for Li Tie. We lost 4-3 which was disappointing but I was delighted to have been on the pitch.

2003

2004

WOLVES v EVERTON 2004

This was my first goal for Everton. The team was struggling at the time but we were safe from relegation so the manager gave me my first start. I scored after two minutes! James McFadden crossed the ball and I was in the right place at the right time to knock it in. We ended up losing 2-1 but it was nice to be on the scoresheet for the first time.

2006

2007

2009

2010

EVERTON v LIVERPOOL 2006

I think every Evertonian would have this in his or her Top Six! We beat Liverpool 3–0 that day and that was a result we hadn't enjoyed in a derby match for decades. Andy Johnson scored twice and Tim Cahill got the other and our fans celebrated for weeks afterwards. That was a great afternoon!

EVERTON v LARISSA 2007

I've picked this game because I scored the club's Goal of the Season in it! We were going well in Europe and we were confident that we'd beat Larissa, which we did 3–1. My moment came just after half-time. Tim Cahill fed Leighton Baines who crossed the ball low and when Steven Pienaar flicked it back, I fired into the bottom corner. It was a goal I really enjoyed!

EVERTON v MANCHESTER UNITED 2009 FA CUP

This was one of the most emotional and incredible afternoons of my career. In truth, it wasn't a great game but to beat Manchester United at Wembley in an FA Cup semi-final is just about as good as it gets. I'm just glad the lads sorted it out on penalties before I had to take one!

EVERTON v CHELSEA 2010

We'd waited a long time to beat Chelsea and to do it at Goodison after going a goal behind was special. Louis Saha had a great game that night and terrorised John Terry all match, scoring both our goals. We proved on that occasion just how good we can be; and we did it again the week after when we beat Manchester United

SYLVAIN DISTIN
Defender

SPOT THE DIFFERENCE

CAN YOU FIND 8 DIFFRENCES IN PICTURE 1?

PICTURE 1

PICTURE 2

Answers on Page 61

EX-FACTOR

LIKE AT EVERY FOOTBALL CLUB, MANAGERS AT EVERTON HAVE COME AND GONE OVER THE DECADES; WITH VARYING DEGREES OF SUCCESS.

HARRY CATTERICK

(1961-1973)

Two league titles, an FA Cup and two Charity Shields were the reward for Harry Catterick's dedication and commitment to Everton. A no-nonsense workaholic, he was ahead of his time in terms of what he expected from his players on and off the pitch and it helped bring many happy times to Goodison Park!

BILLY BINGHAM

(1973-1977)

Another ex-Blue, Bingham found his way back to Goodison when he replaced his former boss, Harry Catterick. Unfortunately, the team no longer boasted the talents it did when he won the title as a player in 1963 and a fourth-place League finish was his greatest achievement.

COLIN HARVEY

(1987-1990)

Colin Harvey, a legend during his playing days with the Club, had the tricky task of taking over when Howard Kendall departed for the first time in 1987. He got off to a fantastic start, winning the Charity Shield thanks to a victory over Coventry City at Wembley, and later led us back there to play in the 1989 FA Cup final against Liverpool.

MIKE WALKER

(1994)

Mike Walker had performed wonders with unfashionable Norwich City so his arrival in January 1994 had all our fans excited. And it all started brilliantly thanks to a massive 6-2 win over Swindon at Goodison. Sadly, it was a rare high and Walker lasted just 10 months in the job.

SOME HAVE GUARANTEED THEIR NAMES AND ACHIEVEMENTS WILL BE PASSED DOWN THROUGH GENERATIONS OF EVERTONIANS, WHILE SOME HAVE LEFT WISHING THINGS COULD HAVE TURNED OUT JUST A LITTLE BIT DIFFERENTLY. HERE'S A RUNDOWN OF SOME OF THE MEN WHO HAVE TAKEN THE REINS OF OUR GREAT CLUB, INCLUDING SOME YOU WILL KNOW; AND SOME YOU MAY NOT.

GORDON LEE
(1977-1981)

Gordon Lee arrived at Goodison with a superb track record and lived up to his reputation by taking a relegation-threatened Everton to a top-half finish and the League Cup final in his first season. He also steered the Blues to third and fourth-place League finishes during his four years in charge.

HOWARD KENDALL
(1981-1987, 1990-1993, 1997-1998)

All those dates above aren't misprints... Howard Kendall really did manage Everton three times! He will forever be remembered for his first stint in charge though, when he oversaw the Club's most successful ever era, winning two League titles, an FA Cup and the European Cup Winners' Cup.

JOE ROYLE
(1994-1997)

A striker who made his Everton debut aged just 16, Joe Royle was a Goodison Park favourite during the late 1960s and early 1970s. He ensured his contribution as a manager would also never be forgotten by steering the Blues to an incredible FA Cup victory over Manchester United in 1995.

WALTER SMITH
(1998-2002)

Walter Smith arrived at Everton with a big reputation having enjoyed huge success as the manager of Glasgow Rangers. After an up and down few seasons for the Toffees, the Scot set about putting things right again but a lack of transfer funds made it difficult to build a side which could challenge for top honours.

KEVIN SHEEDY IS A GENUINE EVERTON LEGEND!

'**S**heeds' is an Academy coach at Everton these days and with a wealth of playing and coaching experience under his belt he's an ideal role-model for the boys who have aspirations of making it through the ranks and into the first-team.

There's plenty of talent about but as Kevin says, it's a long way from the Academy to the Premier League.

"Yes it is and there is a lot of hard work to be done before any young player can even think about being a part of David Moyes' plans," he said. "But we've got a great set-up here at Finch Farm with some great coaches looking after the boys so we're giving them every chance of realising their dream. And, of course, we've got a first-team manager who is always willing to give youth an opportunity, which helps."

David Moyes has certainly never been one to shy away from selecting young footballers in his teams. Jack Rodwell, James Vaughan and Victor Anichebe have all broken into his plans in recent seasons and Moyes was the man who gave a certain Wayne Rooney his Premier League debut back in 2002.

The manager's motto is 'if they're good enough, they're old enough' and that's music to the ears of the Academy coaches.

"The manager here is brilliant with the way he deals with young players," he said. "I know myself from my days of being a young professional that you need guidance, discipline and encouragement at various different times."

Sheedy was a teenager himself when he made his debut for Hereford United and he impressed so much at Edgar Street that he was signed by a big First Division club in 1978: Liverpool!

Things didn't work out at Anfield and so he was delighted to cross Stanley Park in 1982 and join the Howard Kendall revolution at Goodison Park.

"I had no doubts about leaving Liverpool for Everton," he recalled. "To be fair Liverpool were winning the League and European Cups at the time so it was always going to be easier for me to get some regular football at Everton. Fortunately, Howard Kendall was in the process of building a wonderful team and my Everton career ended up being better than I could ever have expected."

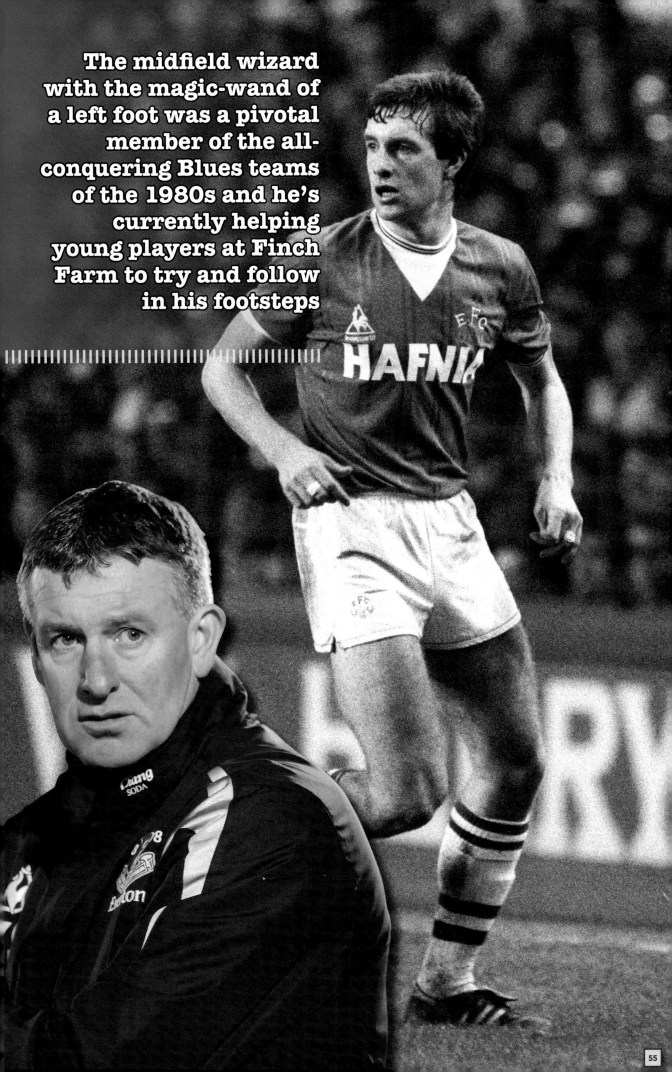

The midfield wizard with the magic-wand of a left foot was a pivotal member of the all-conquering Blues teams of the 1980s and he's currently helping young players at Finch Farm to try and follow in his footsteps

18 78

NIL SATIS NISI OPTIMUM

Everton

EVERTON LADIES

While there may have been no silverware for the first-team during the 2009/10 campaign, the ever-impressive Everton Ladies made sure some room had to be found in Goodison Park's trophy cabinet!

MO

Marley's side went all the way to the FA Women's Cup final and won the competition for the first time in their history thanks to a dramatic 3-2 extra-time win over Arsenal.

The Ladies, whose home ground is Marine FC's Arriva Stadium, were known as Leasowe Pacific until 1995, when they linked up with Everton to improve their chances of success. It worked and three years later they won their first ever League title!

Unfortunately, Arsenal's brilliance since that time means our Ladies are still looking for their second championship triumph - though winning the FA Cup certainly suggests they're heading in the right direction!

In fact, cup competitions aside, the Ladies have finished runners-up to the Gunners in the league in each of the last five seasons, making them one of the most feared teams in the women's game.

Such success means Marley's side have also been granted a shot at European football in recent years, allowing them to test themselves against some of the biggest teams countries such as Norway, Germany and Sweden have to offer.

Winning the FA Cup last season was a fantastic achievement which left Evertonians everywhere proud to be associated with the team. And here's what our victorious Ladies had to say about it;

"It's definitely the best feeling ever. To end up winning the game with a late goal is just the best feeling I've ever had in my life. I thought it was definitely destined for penalties and if anything, Arsenal looked like they were going to score. And then we just had a break away, the goalkeeper, Emma Byrne, has come out and I saw her and dinked it over. I just jumped into the crowd - I don't even know if they were our fans or not!" **NATASHA DOWIE**

"It's just unbelievable. We've been threatening for a few years now to win competitions and this was the icing on the cake. A few people have questioned whether we've got the winning mentality, but now we've proved we have." **MO MARLEY**

"I don't think I can actually put it into words. I'm amazed that we've been able to get the result, which I think we deserved on the day. We had plenty of chances and I just think we were very resilient towards the end and held out for the win." **RACHEL BROWN**

PLAYER PROFILES

YAKUBU AYEGBENI

Nigerian powerhouse Yakubu joined Everton from Middlesbrough in August 2007 for what was then a club record £11.25million fee. An instant hit, 'Yak' became the first player since Peter Beardsley in 1992 to score 20 goals in a season. An international with over 50 caps, an Achilles injury kept him out for much of the following campaign but he returned for the 2009/10 season and again demonstrated his excellent movement and lethal predatory instincts.

VICTOR ANICHEBE

Lagos-born Anichebe is a powerful and pacy striker who broke through from Everton's Academy system to make his first-team debut against Chelsea in January 2006. A star of the Blues' 2007/08 UEFA Cup run, a serious knee injury ruined his 2008/09 campaign, but he fought back to regain a place in David Moyes' squad last term. A Nigerian international, Victor won a silver medal at the 2008 Olympics in Beijing.

JAMES VAUGHAN

A player who has been on our books since the age of nine, Vaughan remains the Premier League's youngest-ever scorer having notched a debut goal against Crystal Palace aged 16 years and 271 days. And, but for a succession of injuries, we would certainly have seen the England Under-21 international in the Blue of Everton more often than we have! James went in search of valuable first-team experience last season and enjoyed loan spells at Derby County and Leicester City!

JOAO SILVA

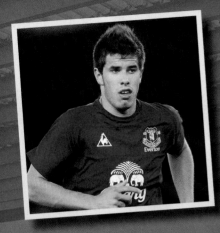

Everton signed Silva from Portuguese side Desportivo Das Aves in June 2010. The striker, who penned a three-year deal, arrived on Merseyside having scored 14 goals in 32 appearances for Aves during the 2009/10 campaign – his first in professional football. A Portugal Under-20 international, the Blues reportedly beat a number of top clubs to the signature of the 6ft 2ins frontman and his first appearance for the Blues came in the pre-season win over Australian A-League side Melbourne Heart.

MAGAYE GUEYE

French Under-21 international Gueye joined Everton from homeland club RC Strasbourg in the summer of 2010. A winger or a striker, the youngster burst on to the scene in France by scoring in each of Strasbourg's first five games of the 2009/10 season. His campaign was then rocked by a succession of injuries, but that didn't stop him starting brightly for the Blues – he scored a winner against Australian side Brisbane Roar in just his third appearance for David Moyes' side! Magaye has followed in the footsteps of his father, Souleymane, who was also a footballer and an international for Senegal!

LOUIS SAHA

French international Saha joined Everton from Manchester United in the summer of 2008 for an undisclosed fee. A winner of two Premier League titles and an FA Cup during his four-and-a-half years at Old Trafford, his spell there was also blighted by a succession of injuries. Rejuvenated since his move to Merseyside, 'King Louis' scored after just 25 seconds of the 2009 FA Cup final – the fastest-ever Wembley final goal – and was a regular on the scoresheet during the 2009/10 campaign.

the EVERTON FOUNDATION

Zip-sliding, mountain climbing, assault courses, bungee jumping... all sounds like fun, doesn't it?

Well, these are the types of activities that the Everton Foundation organise to raise money to support a large number of local sports-related activities and programmes.

The Everton Foundation has been running as an independent charity since June 2004 (when it was known as Everton In The Community) and has since raised huge sums which have gone towards helping people of all ages, backgrounds and abilities across Merseyside.

Did you know that thanks to the Everton Foundation and their top-level coaches, we have one of the most successful blind football teams in Britain? Our wheelchair football team has also tasted glory at tournaments across the country and these are just two examples of successful projects the Everton Foundation run.

Other activities have even had David Moyes' first-team players involved, meaning hundreds of young Evertonians have been fortunate enough to meet one or more of their Goodison heroes. As you can see from our pictures, one lucky Blue even got to take on Sylvain Distin at table tennis.

And the best bit is YOU can get involved. Whether you're a daredevil, a keen sportsperson or just somebody who wants to help out where you can, the Everton Foundation is sure to offer something that's right up your street.

Volunteering to help the Everton Foundation or simply pledging to raise funds is a great way to help your Club and help Everton improve the lives of football fans across the region – fans who may not be as lucky as yourself.

To find out more about the Everton Foundation, visit their website evertonfoundation.org.

QUIZ ANSWERS

JUNIOR QUIZ PAGE 20

1) Hamilton Academical or Dunfermline Athletic; 2) Hull City; 3) They were both in stoppage time; 4) Marseilles; 5) They have all played for Glasgow Rangers; 6) Manchester United and Tottenham Hotspur; 7) Lisbon, Portugal; 8) Sunderland and Hull City; 9) The Harlem Globetrotters; 10) Leeds United; 11) Leeds United; 12) False - Jamie Ashdown was in goal for Portsmouth; 13) Alan Irvine; 14) Petr Cech; 15) Philippe Senderos, Landon Donovan, Per Koldrup and Wayne Rooney.

SO, DO YOU DO KNOW YOUR HISTORY... ? Page 39

1. 1878; 2. 1890/91; 3. Dixie Dean; 4. Harry Catterick was the manager and we defeated Sheffield Wednesday 3–2; 5. The Holy Trinity; 6. Bob Latchford; 7. The European Cup Winners' Cup; 8. Paul Rideout; 9. Walter Smith; 10. Chelsea

WORDSEARCH PAGE 27

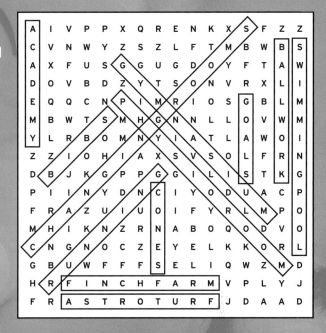

SPOT THE DIFFERENCE PAGE 51